To my sardines, Merret and Harlan,
with all my love.

A Feiwel and Friends Book

An imprint of Macmillan Publishing Group, LLC

120 Broadway, New York, NY 10271

mackids.com

Our books may be purchased in bulk for promotional, educational, or business use.

Please contact your local bookseller or the Macmillan Corporate and Premium Sales Department

at (800) 221-7945 ext. 5442 or by e-mail at MacmillanSpecialMarkets@macmillan.com.

Library of Congress Cataloging-in-Publication Data is available.

First edition, 2021

Book design by Mike Burroughs

Book illustrations were digitally collaged in Photoshop using scanned monoprints and sketches.

Feiwel and Friends logo designed by Filomena Tuosto

Printed in China by RR Donnelley Asia Printing Solutions Ltd., Dongguan City, Guangdong Province.

ISBN 978-1-250-77708-9 (hardcover)

1 3 5 7 9 10 8 6 4 2

A Troop of Kangaroos

Lisa Mundorff

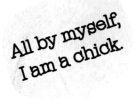

All by myself,
I am a chick

Along come
some friends
and . . .

Feiwel and Friends

New York

We become a
chattering of chickens.

A group of us are a
stench of skunks.

All together, we're a
troop of kangaroos.

A lot of us together become a
party of jays.

When we're hanging out, we're a **camp of bats**.

When we're more than a few, we're a
business of ferrets.

When we wander in a group, we're a **parade of elephants**.

When we huddle together, we're a **float of crocodiles**.

When we gather, we become a
family of sardines.

And when we all
come together with love,
we are a community.

Who are we?

More clever group names
for our animal friends.

Tower of Giraffes

Charm of Hummingbirds

Wisdom of Wombats

Blessing of Narwhals

Band of Coyotes

Nursery of Raccoons